Let's look at the Hedge

Concept by Claude Delafosse
Produced by Gallimard Jeunesse
Written by Caroline Allaire
Illustrated by Pierre de Hugo

FIRST DISCOVERY CLOSE-UPS

MOONLIGHT PUBLISHING

Hedgehog

A hedgehog's back is prickly because it is covered in spines, which are sharp as needles and full of lice.

Whenever it feels threatened it sticks out its prickles and rolls into a ball. Hedgehogs live alone and move around mostly at night.

A hedgehog is omniverous; it eats everything: insects, caterpillars, centipedes, slugs, snails, mice, baby birds and snakes.

On the last page of this book,
you'll find your magnifying glass. Slip it around the plastic pages with the open part in front and the closed part behind.
As you move it around little by little you will discover all about the creatures that live in the hedge!

Are you ready to find out
what you can discover in the hedge ?
Well then, let's go and take a close look at

a hedgehog,
a robin,
a butterfly,
a beetle,
a fieldmouse
a snail

and you'll see them as you have never seen them before !

A hedge is an enclosure like a fence but instead of stakes and wire it is made of bushes, thorns and branches woven together. Hedges mark boundaries but also give shelter from the wind. Because they often have an embankment and a ditch, hedges help to drain the fields.

Many animals live in hedges, where they can find the food they need.

Hedgehog

 A hedgehog's back is prickly because it is covered in spines, which are as sharp as needles and full of lice.

 Whenever it feels threatened, it sticks out its prickles and rolls up into a ball. Hedgehogs live alone and move around mostly at night.

 A hedgehog is omniverous; it eats everything: insects, caterpillars, centipedes, slugs, snails, mice, baby birds and snakes!

Robin

A bold, rather aggressive character, the robin does not hesitate to square up to any bird or other small invader of its territory .

It normally feeds on insects and worms but will often come into gardens especially in winter in search of food.

It likes to sit on low branches or hop around on the ground watching over the patch of hedge or garden it considers to be its own.

Peacock Butterfly

This butterfly feeds on nectar from flowers; it uses its feelers to smell, touch and recognize different flowers.

Its wings are covered in thousands of tiny, coloured scales, all perfectly arranged to form beautiful patterns.

The female butterfly lays her eggs on the leaves of nettles, on which the caterpillars will feed when they hatch out.

Peacock Butterfly

 This butterfly feeds on nectar from flowers; it uses its feelers to smell, touch and recognize different flowers.

 Its wings are covered in thousands of tiny, coloured scales, all perfectly arranged to form beautiful patterns.

 The female butterfly lays her eggs on the leaves of nettles, on which the caterpillars will feed when they hatch out.

Rose-beetle

 You will find this beetle on flowers, where it does not collect nectar like bees, but devours the stamens and pistils and even the petals.

 The hard, protective body shell of the rose-beetle reflects and flashes colour in the sunlight like a precious stone.

 The sides of its wing covers have indents, so that it can use its wings with the covers almost closed. It buzzes loudly as it flies.

Rose-beetle

You will find this beetle on flowers, where it does not collect nectar like bees, but devours the stamens and pistils and even the petals.

The hard, protective body shell of the rose-beetle reflects and flashes colour in the sunlight like a precious stone.

The sides of its wing covers have indents, so that it can use its wings with the covers almost closed. It buzzes loudly as it flies.

Fieldmouse

 A fieldmouse eats seeds, buds, insects and fruit. Its teeth are strong enough for it to gnaw holes in wood!

 It is a good climber and can occupy the nest of a bird of prey or a squirrel's dray! It is hard to see because it comes out at night.

 If threatened, it uses its strong back legs to leap out of the way. If you try to grab it by the tail, it slips out of your hand and escapes.

Snail

It has a funny head with its little feelers sticking up like horns. The two little round balls on the ends of these are its eyes.

Its shell protects it from the sun, the wind and the rain but it is also acts as its lungs because it lets air into the hollow inside.

It leaves a shiny trail of saliva, which helps it grip on to things and to slide along. Saliva blocks up the entrance to its shell in winter.

Spider

Small tortoiseshell
butterfly

Earthworm

You have been able to look close up
at some of the animals that live in
hedges. There are many more.

Ants always seem to be busy
carrying seeds, dead insects and bits
of leaves back to the anthill. They
use their feelers to send messages
to one another.

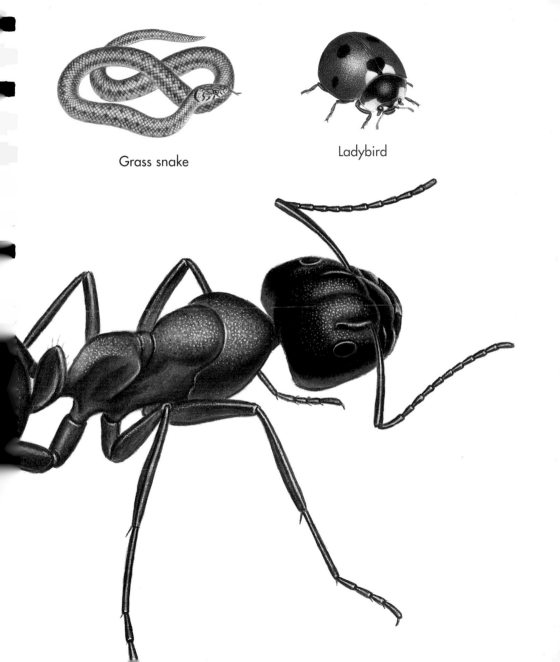

Grass snake

Ladybird

Tawny owl

Buzzard

Toad

Rabbit

Partridge

Foxes eat rabbits, fieldmice and other small animals, but when food is scarce, especially in winter, they will kill hens, ducks and geese and steal from dustbins.

FIRST DISCOVERY: OVER 100 TITLES AVAILABLE IN FIVE SERIES

Translator: Penelope Stanley-Baker
ISBN 1 85103339 4
© 2002 by Editions Gallimard Jeunesse
English text © 2003 by Moonlight Publishing Ltd
First published in the United Kingdom 2003
by Moonlight Publishing Limited, The King's Manor, East Hendred, Oxon. OX12 8JY
Printed in Italy by Editoriale Lloyd